South Shields

in old picture postcards volume 1

by D. Johnson

European Library

ZALTBOMMEL/THE NETHERLANDS

GB ISBN 90 288 3004 9

© 1985 European Library – Zaltbommel/The Netherlands

Fifth edition, 1998: reprint of the original edition of 1985.

Visitors to South Shields are often surprised to find how old the town really is and how much of the original attractive countryside still surrounds it. The origins of the town stretch back even before the coming of the Romans, and flint weapons were found beneath the level of the Roman station and at Tyne Dock.

The Roman Fort itself was founded about 80 A.D. The site was of great strategic significance, at the mouth of a navigable river and dominating a long stretch of coast line, as well as being the probable terminus of one of the four roads in the area, the Wrekendyke.

Numerous relics of the Roman occupation still exist, among the most touching being the gravestone of a Regina, a local woman, wife of Barates. He was probably a merchant from Palmyra, an important trading city. Thus we see not only the early beginnings of South Shields as a commercial port but also the tradition of good race relations! The Roman Fort appears to have been occupied until the Romans left Britain early in the fifth century, but there is evidence that by A.D. 364, Saxon invaders were harrying the coast and it is not surprising that they in their turn also took advantage of the Lawe Top site.

King Oswald appears to have had one of his royal seats at South Shields, and tradition gives the birthplace of his son Oswin as South Shields, or Caer Urfa as it was then. Oswin gave St. Hilda the land for a church about 647-648, which was later named after her, this makes St. Hilda's the site of one of the earliest Christian churches in the north. Further waves of invaders from Scandinavia again harried the coast, and in A.D. 787 and 794 they plundered the nearby monastery of St. Paul's, east Jarrow.

Here we have perhaps the first mention of shipwrecks and the Herd Sand, as traditionally part of the Viking fleet was lost there. A.D. 865 and again 875 saw them returning in force but they were driven out of Durham about 883 by Guthard, who had been invested with the royal insignia as King of Northumbria on the Lawe Top.

The independent northerners, who did not take kindly to the Norman Conquest, rebelled against their rulers. The new King William came north in 1069 and quashed the uprising with fire and sword. So thorough was he that the northern counties were not included in the Domesday Book. Those who were left were not only in danger from famine but also from the marauding Scots who took the able-bodied back to their homes as slaves. But once again the site attracted the hardy survivors, there was fish to be had from the Tyne and a small huddle of huts made its appearance on the river bank near the Lawe.

What was left of the fort was possibly destroyed by the Danes, in 870. If not then, William's troops would have made short work of any fortifications useful to rebels. The fisher folk appear to have preferred their convenient riverside haunts to the windy hill top. They were not at the mercy of any lord of the manor, however, but were, and had claimed to be since 882, the people of the church, and were subject to the rule of the Bishop of Durham.

The earliest mention of South Shields by something near its modern name is in 1235 in the Melsanby Buke where South Scheles makes an appearance. At this time Harton and Westoe were separate villages; the village of Harton being just as important as its neighbours and having a chapel dedicated to St. Lawrence. With the shift of style of government in England and the movement from links with Scandinavia to links with France from 1066 comes a lessening of the strategic and economic importance of the Lawe site. This would continue until the Civil War and the rise of the coal-glass-chemical trade. The little village was in a cul-de-sac, while armies marched to Scotland via Newcastle and to London and the south coast ports to France via York.

The civil strife of the Wars of the Roses and the long-running feud with the Scots appear to have made little mark locally, though the fact that the monks of Jarrow unanimously decided to give a donation to Richard of Gloucester's puninitive raid on Scotland in 1482 seems to point to a knowledge of the dangers of Scottish raids in the area.

The first known map of the South Shields area was drawn in

1509 and South Shields was also 'on the map' as far as local Catholics were concerned, because a centre for smuggling priests into the country from the continent had been established here during Elizabeth I's reign.

A less controversial trade was in local salt and by the mid-sixteenth century there were 153 salt pans in South and North Shields. During the Civil War the Lawe Top fortifications were the site of brisk action. The Tyne was originally in Royalist hands and was one of their principal means of communication with the continent. The Roundhead Scots attacked the fort on 15th and 16th March 1644, then finally on the 20th the Royalists were forced to flee across to Tynemouth, leaving fort, ordnance, ammunition and colours in the hands of the Scots. It was re-taken three months later by Montrose and Sir John Marley, Mayor of Newcastle. The Roundheads would not be beaten, and finally took the fort in July and the fall of Newcastle and Tynemouth Castle in October virtually ended the Civil War in the north.

St. Hilda's vestry minute books of 1660-61 tell of Shieldsmen ruined because of the war, and accounts of the time speak of villages burned to the ground and the countryside laid waste. Evidence also appears of the continuing importance of the salt-making industry. Many of the salt manufacturers were also Quakers and Baptists and three were accused and arrested in 1664 for plotting a rebellion but the matter died down.

Again in 1666 the town was placed on a defensive footing during the war with Holland, Denmark and France and the local men volunteered to defend their town but their help was not needed.

The eighteenth century saw the gradual creeping in of industrialisation. Salt manufacturing continued to be important, and was joined by the mining and export of coal, the manufacture of glass, the building and repairing of ships, with a host of secondary industries such as rope making and the baking of biscuits for provisions on board ships. During the Jacobite rebellions of 1715 and 1745, the ferries plus all guns and arms were seized but again these measures proved un-

necessary. It was not until 1768 that the South Shields that we know began to take shape, when the Market Place was laid out, and the old Town Hall with the streets immediately surrounding it were built. There is not a great deal of difference between the maps of South Shields in 1768 and 1827, but by the time the surveyors for the first Ordnance Survey maps of the area, published in 1857, were at work, housing for the workers flooding in to Tyneside was beginning to fill in the triangle of available land. The great movement of labour away from agriculture and the villages to towns and industry radically changed the borough.

Census records show the influx of workers and their families from Scotland, Ireland, Norfolk and the adjoining counties of Northumberland and Cumberland as well as Scandinavia. Local mining and shipbuilding together with construction work on new docks, houses, public buildings, shops, railways and so forth, swallowed up this army of workers and moulded them into Geordies.

Local government responded to the needs of the growing town by the provision of public baths in 1854, numerous schools in the 1870's, a public library in 1873, the Marine Parks in 1890, and a slum clearance programme with new housing estates in the 1920's and 30's. The expanding town obtained a Charter of Incorporation on 3rd September 1850, and became a county borough on the 1st of April, 1889 Westoe Village became part of South Shields in 1897 but it still retains its own character and charm. The village of Harton followed in 1921 and the borough boundaries were again extended in 1936 and 1950. On local government reorganisation in 1974 South Shields became part of South Tyneside in the new county of Tyne and Wear.

The town has produced a surprising number of writers of international fame: James Kirkup, James Mitchell and Catherine Cookson, also the inventor of the lifeboat, William Wouldhave, and the first Prime Minister of New Zealand, Sir William Fox. South Tyneside was awarded the Council of Europe flag of honour for 1981, for its town twinning involvement.

1. The old volunteers coming from Trow Rocks along Ocean Road after their annual camp, early in the 1900's. The first volunteer corps in the town were the South Shields Loyal Volunteers, raised in 1797, in response to the threat of invasion by Napoleon. Armed with old flint-lock muskets, with which it was considered good shooting to score a bull's eye at eighty yards, the volunteers met in the Market Place on Sunday afternoons and marched to the Bents for 'Prussian Exercise'. The old English Long Bow was a much deadlier and more accurate weapon than the clumsy musket, but the Shield's men had a good reputation with the flint-lock, besides which they probably did not have the muscles their forebears had to pull a bow.

2. Wapping Street about 1888 with the houses with niches (see top centre). These were supposed to have been built by Flemish weavers fleeing from persecution and the niches were to hold small statues. A less welcome visitor to these shores was the cockroach, supposed to have been brought to this part of the country amongst ballast. Certainly, in the 1880's Brockie says that 'many houses in Shields are full of Cockroaches, especially in cupboards near ovens'. They were once fancied to bring good luck to a house, but a lady in Westoe Village got a breed of them on purpose, and the house was soon over-run. The grocer's shop is owned by T.F. Beadnell, and at number 61 is the shop of Dorothy Sahsa, a curious name which could indicate an early member of the Arab Community.

3. The corner of Fowler Street, east side looking north, in the early 1920's. On the far left we can see the Scala, then the Royal Hotel (now the Ship and Royal), then the Criterion, Oliver's, and finally Goldman's general dealer's shop, with Pearlman's above. The Scala changed to the Gaumont and has recently become an amusement centre; the two pubs are still there, Goldman's has been gone for some time but Oliver's, without the lamps but with a comprehensive collection of tobaccos, cigars and cigarettes, survived until quite recently. By the late sixties, with its dark unchanged interior, and wooden floor, it was so old fashioned that it was something of a period piece. The staff were very obliging, and its demise must have been keenly regretted by many. The shop next door was kept for many years by Mrs. Oliver, the wife of Jack Oliver who ran the tobacconists. It was a sweet shop and Mrs. Oliver must have been a 'sweet' lady, for she was fondly remembered by her customers.

4. Taken about 1898, this shows the Mill Dam end of East Holborn, looking from Coronation Street and Brewery Lane. Note the flat caps, also the bowler hat which was the traditional headwear for the foreman. Brewery Lane commemorates the breweries in this area. The Mill Dam was originally the opening of another mouth of the Tyne which ran along Coronation Street, Catherine Street and out via Ocean Road to the sea. By Napoleonic times this had silted up and after the Napoleonic wars the small creek was filled in as relief work for the unemployed.

5. Crofton's Corner and the Market Place in the 1920's. A very peaceful scene in direct contrast to the night of 2nd October 1941, when a stick of bombs which was dropped over the market place caused some of the worst damage of that terrifying night. The Tram Hotel, the Grapes Hotel, Jackson's the Tailors and the King's Shoe Shop, were gutted, had it not been for the solidity of the dividing walls at Liptons' and Masons' shops, the fire might have caused much more damage in King Street, Crofton's Drapery Stores at the corner of King Street started to burn from a leaking gas main and was soon no more. The fire spread to Woolworth's which was shortly a ruin. By daylight on Friday 3rd, much of what one sees here had been swept away, like a pile of child's building blocks.

6. Albion Street taken about 1914, when the town council were making efforts to demolish the worst of the slums. Far left shows the outside of a privy midden with a pool of water close by, a breeding ground for various diseases. Note the close proximity of the houses in the centre of the picture, also unhealthy. The Public Health Act of 1875 made regulations to stop this type of crowding but this was bolting the stable door after the horse had gone as by this time much cheap housing had been built for the workers who poured in from the country, from Ireland and from Scotland into Tyneside to find work.

7. This quaint building is Trinity Towers, taken about 1880. It was built in 1810, as a pilot's look out. When the Marine parks were opened in 1890, it was taken over as a park-keepers lodge. It was later used by the Education Department and was demolished in 1971. A cairn stands on the site with the crest on the tower cemented to the side. The wording is 'Deus Dabit Vela' (God will give the sails) then 'erected by the master and brethren of the Trinity House Newcastle Upon Tyne 1810. Simon Danson-Master (illegible) Deputy Master'. Mr. Enoch Thompson proposed to build a replica of the towers in Toronto, Canada, as a meeting place for the local Tyneside colony, but the idea never materialised.

8. Mariner's Cottages taken about 1900. They were built by the South Shields Master Mariner's Annuity Society as homes for aged members or widows and orphans of members of the society. The foundation stone for the first five cottages was laid on 7th December 1843 by Robert Anderson, and the buildings were paid for by Dr. Winterbottom. A second foundation stone was laid by Robert Ingham on 26th March 1846. The 21 cottages on the north side were completed by 1847, and the 17 on the south side in 1862. As well as paying for the first cottages, Dr. Winterbottom constructed and stocked a library, donated a telescope, and endowed the building with over £400 in consols to keep the gardens in good order. The library and telescope have vanished, but the cottages remain.

9. Wapping Street and Stobb's Lane in 1910. Stobb's Lane is the narrow alley in the centre of the photograph. It ran from Wapping Street up to Wellington Street, and must have been just another part of the whole adventure play ground this area must have been to the children, who could always temporarily escape from the consequences of their mischief into one of the empty houses. Nearby at the entrance to the Old Ferry Landing nearby stood a quaint building dating back to at least Stuart times, called 'Noah's Ark' after a carving over the door. In later times it was known as 'Bella Booth's' and was supposed to be haunted. The minister of St. Hilda's was asked to exorcise the place, but it is not on record whether this was done or was successful. It was said by some that smuggled French brandy was the only spirit in the house, but that is another story.

10. The foot of the Long Bank, taken between 1910 and 1930 by Mr. Laws. The photograph has a curiously ghostly air, as well it might, for not only was the Old Noah's Ark pub near, but Jack the Hammer lived here not only in life but after death, according to some. Jack had been a travelling tinker, but had evidently seen better days by his manner and even in old age was still a tall, fine-looking man. He lived and died alone in a house in Long Bank, and his uneasy spirit made its presence felt in an unusual and useful manner, by loud knocking on the gable end of the house as with a hammer. The louder the knocks the more severe the storm which they foretold. An old man was put into the house as caretaker as nobody else would live there. He declared it was all nonsense, but the local sailors firmly believed in Jack the Hammer.

11. Fowler Street with the corner of Burrow Street in 1901. The J.T. Dagleas whose sign you can just see on the far left was a plumber. Burrow Street boasted two pawnbrokers at the time this photograph was taken; T. Blanch at number 9 and A.S. Gompertz at number 11, also A.J. Trippit, who was a bootmaker. History is silent on the origin of the name Burrow Street, but according to Horsley 'the field in which the station at South Shields has stood is called the Lawe, formerly it went by the name of the Burrow Meadow'. There is no confusion on the name Fowler Street, however, for it commemorates the Fowler family who at one time owned land in this area. Fowler's Close was a block of freehold land of about 25¼ acres bounded by Fowler Street on the west. In all probability it was one of the ancient freeholds created in 1324.

12. An artist's impression of the new Town Hall in 1910. The original was used for the invitation cards for the official opening of the building. The tale of the disputes behind the building of the new Town Hall is a long one. The town improvement bill of 1855 empowered the council to alter, enlarge or demolish the old Town Hall, and some were in favour of a new Town Hall on the site of the old Golden Lion Pub. J.C. Stevenson favoured demolition and a public hall in the Market Place with covered markets underneath. These plans fell through as did ones for a new Town Hall on alternative sites round the Market Place. A lease was obtained for the present site in 1875, but it was not until 1905 that the foundation stone was actually laid. The clock chimes on the quarter and on the hour. The words to the chimes are 'Lord, through this hour, be thou my guide, so by thy power, no foot shall slide'.

13. Westoe Cemetery in 1886 showing the old bridge over the railway, and who would think while looking on this peaceful scene that graveyards were the subject of great controversy in the Shields Gazette of 1854-55. The problem was that St. Hilda's Churchyard was full to overflowing, and the Dean and Chapter had first refused to allow Holy Trinity Churchyard to be enlarged, then had changed their minds. The editor of the Gazette was hounding the new burial board with vigour, and an outbreak of cholera made matters worse. In 1856 part of Robert Ingham's farm was bought and the cemetery was laid out. The first interment was a boy James Walker Martin, who had been accidentally drowned. Apparently he had once been playing there and had said he would like to be buried in a certain spot. He had his wish.

14. Westoe House in 1899, formerly 'The Hall', was according to Miss Flagg, the gem of the older houses in Westoe Village. It was built mainly in the eighteenth century, with some fragments from an older house dating from the seventeenth century. These came from a house at the low end of the town, that is Shadwell and Thrift Street area, built by Flemish workmen. Sadly, it was demolished in the late 1950's. Perhaps the most interesting resident was Robert Ingham, first M.P. for South Shields, barrister, attorney general for County Durham, and host to many of the leading lights in law, literature and science at what was then a charming country retreat where from the windows one had an unimpeded view of the North Sea, and Tynemouth Priory. The gardens were also famous, and in 1854 thieves got away with two stones of grapes from one of the hothouses. The Ingham Infirmary is named after Mr. Ingham.

15. Westoe House from Westoe Drive in 1927. Even today, this spot can be still as tranquil and almost rural in its character. This road was made from Horsley Hill Road to join up with the path from the top of Westoe Village about 1880. For many years the northern half of Westoe Park Estate, as it was then known, was open land; it was used as allotments after 1914, and was built over later. The small 'island' once had trees and iron railings. Fairfield, Seacroft, Ingleside and Stanhope House stood to the left of the photograph. Fairfield was demolished and Ingleside became Nightingale House which was a half-way house for the mentally ill and is now to become a rehabilitation centre for drug addicts.

16. Earlier inhabitants knew this as Caston Dyke, then it became Westoe Terrace, then Dean Lane, and finally Dean Road. This photograph was taken before 1910 and shows Tindle House, now the site of the 'Regent' Bingo Hall, formerly the Regent Cinema. The 'Regent' was opened by the Mayor and Mayoress, Alderman and J:W. Watson, in 1935. Unlike many cinemas of the period, it had been mainly built by local firms and the architects were also a local firm, Morton and Sons. The architects had played safe by designing it as a cinema, but with space for variety performances. It is surprising to think that prior to 3rd May 1897, the Parishes of South Shields and Westoe were separate entities.

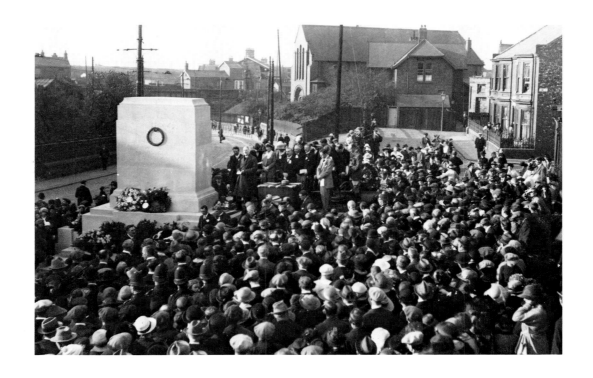

17. The unveiling of Tyne Dock Cenotaph on Saturday 15th October 1921, by Sir Alexander Kaye Butterworth, general manager of the North Eastern Railway Company. It was built from public subscriptions by the West End War Memorial Committee, the chairman being Alderman E.H. Gibbon, who gave an address at the unveiling. He had been in the Third Durham Volunteer Artillery, and had acted as a Recruiting Officer during the war, so in his own words was 'best able to estimate those who rushed to the colours', many of whom this cenotaph commemorates. It is also surprising that he as with many of the committee, do not seem to have seen active service. St. Peter and Paul's Church is shown at the top right, Catherine Cookson, the local authoress, was a member of the congregation in her early years.

18. Wellington Street circa 1900, showing the remains of the old theatre, which stood at the junction of Heron Street and Wellington Street. It was opened in 1792 and closed 1866 when the Theatre Royal, King Street, opened. It was demolished in 1936 prior to the construction of River Drive. Actors famous in their day such as the tragedian MacReady played there and it was owned by the Roxby Beverley family from 1831 until its closure. One programme which survives is for the performance of Miss Clara Fisher from the theatres Royal Covent Garden, and Drury Lane (an infant under eight years of age) on 22nd June 1819 playing the lead in Richard III; three other of the misses Fisher have plum parts in this performance. This was followed by a dance, a song, then the musical entertainment 'Rosina'. Charles Grubb remembers 'the ticket entrance coloured with red ochre. Up a few steps are the boxes, nearly on a level with the pit, with only one tier. Drama followed by an interlude, or singing and dancing and a farce often kept us amused till past midnight'.

19. Field House, situated at the top of Salmon Street, in 1890, and looking like a set from a murder mystery of the 1930's, but it was the 1830's when the house was connected with the death of a magistrate at Jarrow Slake. On 11th June 1832 Ralph Armstrong and William Jobling allegedly seriously injured the owner of the house, Nicholas Fairles. Jobling was brought here to be identified by the dying Fairles, and was later hanged for his murder. Curiously enough, Jobling's wife Isabella had been a servant in the house before her marriage. The land was bought for housing in 1902, and the name Fairles Street is now the only reminder of the house and the once important family.

20. The end of Military Road and Mile End Road, showing the Greens' Sailor Boys home. It stood on the site of the old Fairles family home. The house was originally built by Thomas Barker, shipowner, and was known as Mile End House. About 1825 it passed into the possession of the Green family, who resided there for many years. In 1877 the premises were presented by the Reverend Robert Green and his sisters to the Wellesley Committee, with the object of providing a home for old Wellesley boys returning from sea. (The Wellesley School-Ship had been set up as a Training School for destitute boys in 1868.) It subsequently became a hospital for the ship then in 1885 was converted into a Junior Branch of the School-Ship, being licensed for sixty boys.

21. The corner of Keppel Street looking north-west in 1900. Note the errand boy at the door of Wetherell's; orders would be delivered to customers in those days. Again, all that you see here was swept away shortly after this photograph was taken, and is in the process of being changed again. Keppel Street was at one time Keppel Lane, home of Thomas Wilson's quarterly school. There is some confusion as to which Keppel the street commemorates, some of the contenders are Admiral Viscount Augustus Keppel who was the second son of the second Earl of Albemarle; the sixth Earl of Albemarle, George Thomas Keppel, who fought at Waterloo; and Admiral Sir Henry Keppel, a famous figure in the Royal Navy in Victorian days.

22. Brinkburn Farm with the commencement of the footpath to Harton Colliery, taken about 1900. The Harton Coal Company had at one time owned the land, and the farmlands and the footpath to the colliery, the type of scenery D.H. Lawrence loved to describe, went within living memory. There had been an eviction wrangle over the house but thankfully in 1978 the house was sold then carefully restored by its present owners. The exact date of building of the house is not known, but there is a building which could possibly be it on a map of the area dated 1768.

23. The lodge at Dean House at the bottom of Dean Road, taken about 1900. People who know this area as it is now may be surprised that this building was actually a lodge of Dean Villa, a house which stood in its own grounds among fields, and the only things to disturb the peace nearby were the two branch lines of the North Eastern Railway which had been built quite recently on either side. Corny Hill, which had been covered and is about to be covered again by housing, stood to the north-east. A winding lane ran past a number of quarries to Westoe; the map of 1768 gives it the ominous title of Cut-Throat Lane but we know it now by a more prosaic name – Dean Road.

24. The home of Joseph Mason Moore, who was a member of the Town Council from 1862 to 1871 when he resigned to become Town Clerk on the death of Thomas Salmon. He was very fond of gardening, chrysanthemums being his favourite flower. Once a year he opened his garden to the public, also providing music and refreshments. This shot must have been taken at one of these open days. The story of the house is a curious one. It stands on the site of J.A. Urwin's shop which was demolished to make way for it. Later the house was converted into shops, the window on the right now faces into Moore Avenue.

25. Floods at the Deans, 1900. Momentarily, the children here are more interested in the photographer than the scene he is trying to capture. It was taken just about opposite Dean House, and the buildings on the left are part of the Dean Brewery which stood on the site of what was the Deans Estate. Earlier in 1900, there had been a disagreement between the owner of the Dean Brewery and the Corporation over the blocking of a sewer; the floods which occurred on Friday 26th and Saturday 27th October 1900, must have made that fade into insignificance. Recommendations were made, and letters were written, but to this day the Tyne Dock area is subject to floods.

26. Frederick Street looking towards Laygate shortly before the First World War. Note the push chair on the left and the barber's pole beside the street lamp. On the right is the Tyne Dock Industrial Co-op, which moved into these premises about 1901. The 'Co-op' had proved particularly popular in the North East where by 1885 'at least one-third of the population purchase their requirements from the Co-operative stores'. As with King Street, the shop fronts have changed, but the upper stories of the buildings are often exactly the same as are shown here. The right-hand side of Frederick Street was the first to be developed, and in the 1850's there were gardens and fields opposite, but by the 1900's the street had developed into a busy shopping centre.

27. The corner of Frederick Street and Laygate Lane in 1906, showing the buildings which were about to be removed for the laying of tramway tracks. The shop on the right is Swords' the printers and the one in the centre is a temperance bar. Temperance bars were quite popular in Victorian and Edwardian South Shields; at the time the photograph was taken there were no less than eight of them in the South Shields directory. By 1940 there were only three and they are now a thing of the past. The church, whose spire is on the right of the picture, is, or was, the Laygate Presbyterian Church which was closed in December 1938 and demolished in early 1959, despite its being designed by John Dobson and having three stained glass windows in memory of the Rennoldson family, as well as a monument to James Stevenson.

28. The Terrace in the South Marine Park about 1929, which was obviously *the* place to see and be seen with the younger set, as the three girls running the gauntlet of the row of young men on the left testifies. The hats seem made for the coy glances, but the open display of silk covered knees by the girl on the steps on the right would have been horrifying to the distinguished throng at the opening of the parks on Race Wednesday in June 1890. Among these in the procession to the new parks were the Knights of Labour, the Temperance Societies, the Smith's Society, and the Society of Railway Servants. The Mayor gave a banquet in the evening at the library hall, and the dinner, of 'A most sumptuous character', was provided by the Royal Hotel.

29. The North Beach in the early 1900's, when the North Pier was being repaired after damage and a new lighthouse built. You can just see the crane to the left on the horizon. Johnson's pleasure boats are lined up ready for customers and the donkey rides already have one prospective jockey. To the right we can see the lifeboat hut built in the early spring of 1867, and not only did it enable the members of the newly formed Volunteer Life Brigade to keep a bad weather watch in comfort, but it provided a quickly accessible source of warmth and comfort to the victims of the depressingly numerous shipwrecks of the time. To the crew of the schooner 'Impulse', wrecked in September 1868, the modest hut must have seemed better than a palace. The cook of the ship had thoughtfully brought a plum-pudding which he had been cooking with him as a housewarming present, however.

30. Cleadon Hills showing the old mill in the middle distance and Cleadon Water Works to the right. A stranger to the area might wonder at the inclusion of this photograph, but to generations of the inhabitants of South Shields, Cleadon Hills was an adventure playground, a place for exercising the dog, doing your courting, playing with your sledge in winter, and so on. The mill itself was possibly built about 1820 and verbal tradition asserts that it was built by the Reverend George Cooper Abbs, of Abbs House, Cleadon Village. It is certainly on the 1854 Ordnance Survey map. It had been disused for 60 or 70 years by 1955 when Sir Robert Chapman reminisced about it. He also remembered farm buildings there and the artillery unit stationed on the site during the First World War.

31. Another fair at the Market Place — note the weighing chair. St. Hilda's Church in the background stands, it is said, on the site of a monastery founded by St. Hilda circa 648. Part of the church may date back to mediaeval times but the main part of the structure was built between 1810 and 1812. St. Hilda's was the only Anglican church in South Shields, until 1819 when St. Thomas' was opened, and until 1870 pews were privately owned. The church was damaged during a particularly severe air raid on the night of 2nd October 1941. All the windows were shattered, the roof dislodged, and the walls pitted and scarred with shrapnel. There are several memorials in the church to various local persons, together with an interesting model of the lifeboat 'Original' suspended from the ceiling. Its inventor, William Wouldhave, lies at rest outside.

32. Part of Corstorphine Town in the 1890's. This was a speculative building venture by the Scot Robert Corstorphine, who built it in 1839, and who was subsequently the landlord of the Cookson's Arms Inn. 'Robby' Corstorphine had also been an employee of Cookson's Chemical Works and had spoken with James Mather at a meeting in support of the works in 1843, when numerous legal actions were making the situation difficult for the owners. The area was absorbed by Readhead's Docks in 1918. The horse tram is on the Tyne Dock route. The men hanging about are probably hoping for work at the nearby docks. It was still customary until the Second World War, for men to wait at the dock gate in the morning, until those found suitable had been picked out.

33. This part of Corstorphine Town was known as Newmarket. It is shown as it was in 1900. The name commemorated the unrealised hope of Mr. James Young, who intended it to be a rival of the market place near St. Hilda's. It was opened in 1857, but never really caught on. The clock was taken out in 1954; despite the fact that it was well known for its accuracy. It had been re-erected on 21st February 1913 and set in motion by the Mayor, Councillor John Watt Henderson. Note the old advertisements, or 'street jewellery', as they are now called, also the coachman complete with top hat.

34. This photograph showing the foot of East Holborn was taken in 1920. The vicar of Holy Trinity notes in 1911 that rolling of lighted tar barrels down this and other of the many banks in old shields was a popular pastime until the 1890's. Whether this was a degraded form of the Shetland New Year custom of lighting tar barrels or not is debatable, certainly men and lads were brought in from Orkney and Shetland in 1824 as strike breakers; and there was also a connection with these islands and the old Tyneside whaling industry and later the herring fleets as well. The name Holborn itself is a relic of the coal trade to London.

35. This shot of East Holborn in the late 1920's gives some idea of the narrowness of the streets, one of the many reasons why it was demolished in the 1930's. It shows the Hop Pole Inn, Polly Milliard's Fish Shop, French's Fruit Shop and Camillieri's Lodging House. This densely populated area had many lodging houses for the sailors who later often settled permanently in the area. The local Medical Officer of Health often had a running battle trying to keep these premises within the law and it must have been a great relief when these frequently neglected streets with their vermin and insect life finally went.

36. Station Road looking north in 1905. The Old Low Railway Station is commemorated by this name, dating back to the days when a passenger's 'coach' was an open truck with low sides, resembling the goods waggons in use to-day, with seats placed in it and a door on each side. On the right the tall tower is the Pigeon Well in St. Hilda's colliery yard. It was given this name because the purity and sweetness of the water made it a favourite drinking place for local pigeons. The well was used to fill, by pumping, the large water tower in St. Hilda's colliery yard.

37. All the fun of the fair at the Market Place, South Shields. The private Act of Parliament which enabled the market place to be laid out also ensured that the towns people had permission to hold two fairs every year; one upon 24th June and one on 5th September. There was also a provision for a market every week on Wednesday. In Victorian times the arrival of the travelling showmen who transported the slides, merry-go-round and shows was a red-letter day for local people. The late 1890's and 1900's saw them incorporating short film shows into their acts, but the demand for travelling shows dwindled and now there is only Newcastle 'Hoppings' to remind us of how things once were.

38. An early shot of King Street, decorated for Queen Victoria's Jubilee in 1887. The 'Welcome to Shields' caption is hung over what is now the Metro bridge but what was then the Railway bridge. Superficially, the scene is entirely different until one looks to the upper stories of the buildings and realises that they have hardly changed. The Edinburgh buildings with the fanciful tower effect at the corner is still there (centre of the photograph) as is the handsome Queen Anne style building opposite, now occupied by the Citizen's Advice Bureau. King Street was not always a totally commercial area, indeed, Sir Charles Mark Palmer, of Palmers of Jarrow fame, was born there on 3rd November 1822.

39. This photograph, taken in 1903, shows King Street and Mile End Road corner with the original 'Scotia'. This was demolished shortly afterwards to enable Mile End Road to be widened and the new Scotia was built 1903-04 by Henry Grieves, showing an art nouveau influence, despite its Edwardian baroque style. Mile End Road had been the original Sunderland Turnpike Road, and was not given its modern name until 1848. The reason for this name caused Miss Flagg some confusion. The suggestion was made that Mile End House, the home of the owner of the land, Sarah Green, was exactly a mile from Sarah's old home in Commercial Road, so Miss Flagg decided that 'it may have been a whimsical title'. Sarah was the elder daughter of Nicholas Fairles, who was fatally injured at Jarrow Slake, during the miners' strike of 1832, and who owned much land on the Lawe Top.

40. Ocean Road Crossing about 1924. Many of the buildings here are basically as they were then but have changed hands and uses. The one to have seen the most dramatic changes is the Scala Picture Hall, on the left. The building that come to be known as the Scala was opened on 4th February 1891, as the Royal Assembly Hall; by 1920 assembly halls were a thing of the past so it was redecorated and opened on 30th September as a luxury cinema. Patrons in later days may be surprised to know that when it opened it had three cafés, a Palm court, and hairdressing rooms for both sexes. By the time the photograph was taken there was also a Scala Billiards Hall. Chief Inspector Quinn is talking to the policeman and the point boy beside them is William Hewson, who later rose to be a Senior Inspector.

41. Waterloo Vale looking south from Barrington Street, in 1925. The state of the houses on the left tells its own tale; soon they will be demolished. Already the corner shop on the right is partially boarded up. Waterloo Vale is mentioned in the earliest directory of South Shields; White's Directory of 1827. Once the residence of customs officers, it also housed James Lackland's Nautical School. Lackland was an old whaler, crippled by frostbite, and was one of the earliest and best teachers of navigation in the town. John Nevison's Private School was also in Waterloo Vale. Now it waits in the shadow of the gasworks for the demolition men.

42. Lower Thames Street in 1910. The young mother in the picture probably only has one room for herself, her husband and her growing family. The wash-house in the backyard will be shared by the other families as will the babies crying, the family arguments, the joys, fears and tears of a close-knit community. Large families of six and over were common, but the infant mortality rate was 111 per 1,000 births. Lower Thames Street ran parallel with the river. Parks had been opened in the 1890's but they were some distance away and the house only has the dismal prospect of the dilapidated wall as a view; if anyone had time to look out, that is. The properties were not demolished until the 1930's, when the young woman would probably be a grand-mother, if she survived.

43. Men outside the Palatine Hotel, Palatine Street in 1920. Despite its venerable appearance, the Palatine Hotel only dates from the 1880's, the first mention of it being in the 1883 directory, when it was managed by Mrs. Ann Burdon. It was by no means unusual for a woman to keep a public house in those days, or for that matter to own a small business. The doors of the pub are firmly closed, which puts the time of taking of the photograph as before eleven in the morning or after three in the afternoon as 'Dora', or the defence of the Realm Act passed during the First World War curtailed drinking hours. As well as being a county, Durham was also the Palatine of the Bishop of Durham, that is he exercised certain priveleges over the area and owned quite a lot of the land. Hence the name Palatine Street.

44. Thompson's Hall in the 1890's, which was one of the mansions of the riverside, which were often occupied by Master Mariners in the coal trade between London and the Tyne. This one got its name from Major Thompson, though according to the births notices in the Shields Monthly Mirror for 1819 when his wife had a daughter there, it was called Hill House. As the rich moved away from the riverside, these large buildings ended up as tenements. These run down properties were never the less lucrative investments for their landlords, as it was not until 1874 that a Medical Officer of Health was appointed and his efforts to improve housing were greatly hampered by the fact that those living in these slums could not afford to pay for better accommodation.

45. Ocean Road looking towards the Pier in the 1920's. Many centuries ago the River Tyne ran along here to the sea. The road takes its name from the old name for the North Sea, the German Ocean, and has the name German Street on the first Ordnance Survey map of the area, published in 1862. The old workhouse stood on the left, on the site now occupied by the North Marine Park and originally called 'Hungry Hole'. It was closed in 1877. The small café which is just behind the Wouldhave Memorial was badly damaged during the raid of the night of 2nd October 1941, as was the roof covering of the 'Tyne' lifeboat and the old boat itself.

46. Shadwell Street from Corporation Staith in 1913, showing back Military Road. No records exist of the founding of Military Road, but it is thought that the Romans used this as a pathway to their fort on the Lawe Top, and later generations would again use it as access to the fortifications occupying the same site. It was also the scene of an ugly incident between the press gang and local men led by Ralph Peel, husband of Dolly, in 1812, during which firearms were used. In 1838 it was built up, and according to Miss Flagg 'the houses on the north side, two-storied facing the street, clung to the bank like swallow's nests, propped up, particularly in later years, by buildings rising from Shadwell Street, and divided, here and there, by chasm – like 'stairs', amongst them the well-known 'Pilot Stairs'. By 1913 Durham University, the owners of properties in the road, dropped their appeal against closing orders, and demolition gangs moved in.

47. Shadwell Street in 1898, showing Salmon's Quay with the Pier for Railway Ballast on the right. The tunnel for the old Ballast Railway is in the centre of the picture just below the wall. The Railway was constructed in 1846 and was built to convey Ballast under Military Road to the hills at the Lawe, going across the site of the Roman Fort. The Ballast was hauled up by a stationary engine near Trinity Towers. These hills were later removed for the laying out of the Marine parks. Salmon's Quay was named after Thomas Salmon, the first town clerk, who was also a local historian and a solicitor. He was involved in moves to obtain Parliamentary representation for South Shields, to establish it as a separate customs port, to create a local Marine board, and to establish a pilotage commission, as well as many other schemes for the benefit of the town.

48. The corner of Salmon's Lane in Shadwell Street taken by R. Hodge in 1892. By the 1890's cameras had become cheap enough to be within the means of the lower middle and upper working classes. Hodge was one of the unknowns but his work was copied by Mr. Willits who was a keen amateur photographer and one of the first to cover this quaint area of South Shields. Much of his work is now in the local history library. He was a school board man, that is he used to check on school attendance, and perhaps he got the inspiration to make a record of the old town while he was trying to winkle out unwilling pupils from this rabbit warren of streets, where families would often live in one room.

49. The Pilot Office in Green's Place, about 1890. The origins of the pilot service in the area must go back many centuries, certainly the first written references to the Tyne Pilot Service are in 1539, in the order book of Trinity House. Originally pilotage was confined exclusively to the members of Trinity House of Newcastle and this privilege was confirmed by a charter of Elizabeth I in 1584. The jurisdiction of Trinity House, Newcastle was extended in 1687 from Whitby to Holy Island, and Trinity Brethren and pilots were relieved of the duty of serving on juries, bearing arms, and impressment in the navy. During the 1860's the pilots rebelled against the rule of Trinity House over their working conditions and broke free in 1865. The Pilot Office was bought in 1885 and the building was recently converted into flats.

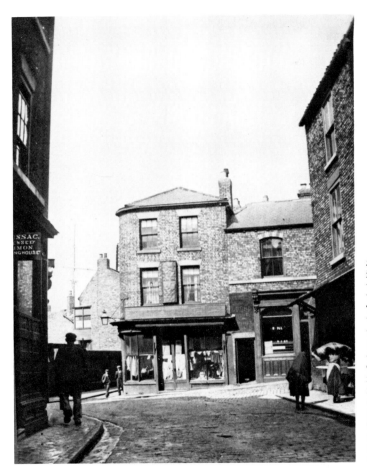

50. The South End of Thrift Street about 1900 showing the entrance to the Bottle and Jug Department of the 'Marquis of Lorne' and a shop described as an 'outfitters' but more probably an old clothes dealer. The 'Bottle and Jug Department' was the old form of 'Off Licence' sales, at one time children could be sent with a porter jug for nanna or granda's pint, but the 1901 Child Messenger Act Limited off-sales to children to one pint in a securely corked or sealed bottle. Curiously enough, there was also a Temperance Hotel in Thrift Street; these were set up by reformers, often in old pubs, but were rarely successful, mainly because of lack of comfort according to one writer. Thrift Street was originally called, appropriately enough, Commerce Street, as many tradesmen such as anchor smiths, coopers, and butchers lived there but by the time this photograph was taken it was mainly pubs, old clothes shops and lodging houses.

51. Thrift Street about 1910 showing the office of Lawson-Batey Tugs, owners of the Black Diamond line of tugs; the Mentor, Nestor, Plover, Royal Briton, Taliesin, Cruiser, Comet, Hercules and Ulysses; the steam signals were two long, four short, one long blast. The vessel which was to become the first tug, the 'Tyne Steamboat', was launched from the south shore at Gateshead on 21st February 1814. A failure as a steamboat passenger vessel, she was re-named the 'Perseverance' and in July 1818 commenced a new and more profitable career as a tug. One famous old tug was the 'Harry Clasper' with an organ that was played by the wind and a figurehead in the likeness of Harry Clasper, the famous oarsman.

52. Coverdale's Quay at the back of Shadwell Street about 1900. This is the back view of the old house with the coat of arms above the door, dating back to Henry VIII's time. One of the women in the picture owned a fish curing business nearby; the combined smells of that and the river in summertime must have been unbelievable. At very high tides the lower part of the backyard used to flood, making access to the W.C. hazardous. The first shipyard in South Shields was near here. Robert Wallis defied Newcastle Corporation, bought the site in 1729 and began building; threats and law suits were met with a spirited opposition, which included tipping a Newcastle alderman into the river.

53. Pan Ash Quay about 1900, taken from the river, showing Crisp and Hail's Marine Stores, Sanderson's Works, and Dixon's Shipsmiths and Windmill Pump Manufacturers. The name is obviously derived from the salt industry, ashes from the salt pans being dumped here. The pans in question were believed to have been those operating off Wapping Street. They were the property of Lewis Frost, one of the leading residents in South Shields in the seventeenth century. It took 50 cwt of coal to produce a ton of salt, an uneconomic proportion which eventually led to the demise of the industry locally.

54. Tyne Dock just before the First World War. This was the first time that rope slings were used to lift a car aboard a ship. The slings were made by James Chalmers, the dock gate-man; one of the many examples of local ingenuity which history books are silent on. On the right is a policeman, and people may have been lulled into believing that this was a law-abiding era. In fact, 'a dozen fights in progress at the same time in the market place was not unusual' according to the Shields Gazette. Work on the Tyne Dock was begun on 3rd March 1856, and the first vessel to enter the completed dock on 22nd January 1859, was the brig 'Recovery' of South Shields. The formal opening by Lord Ravensworth and the Earl of Carlisle was on 3rd March 1859. The Parish of St. Mary's, Tyne Dock, was formed out of the profits from the sale of the land for the dock, Trow Rocks and the site of the South Pier.

55. One of the many Victory teas which took place in 1919. This one is in Waterloo Vale, and the Mayor and Mayoress, Councillor and Mrs. Sykes, are to be seen on the far left of the table at the bottom of the photograph. The table on the right is graced with two aspidestras, and a lady photographer is taking a shot of the helpers in their pinnies. But there is also a vacant chair at the top table where the Mayor and Mayoress are, perhaps an accidental symbol of all those who would not come back to homes which were not fit for anyone, let alone heroes. Mr. R. Buglass, a wine merchant and police superintendent T. Richardson, once lived there, but by 1919 this was a slum area.

56. The tug 'Washington' off Broad Landing in 1910. Perhaps the girls on the right were hoping to find treasure, for in May 1778 as the collier 'John and Mary' was casting her ballast at Cookson's Quay, several silver coins were discovered. Further examination yielded a large number of gold coins of Henry VIII's time. Certainly in the late 1750's Mr. Burdon had obtained a licence for a Ballast Wharf here, and Broad Landing was enlarged in 1832 in exchange for the giving up by the public of Long Row landing to the Stanhope and Tyne Rail Road Company. Even in 1850 it was one of only four public landings available in South Shields for small boats.

57. The brig 'Ann' of Guernsey which was wrecked on the Groyne during the gale of 8th February 1883. The 'Ann' had sailed from the Tyne with a cargo of coal when she ran into a south-easterly gale and was forced to return for shelter. She broached to in the harbour and went ashore, but the crew were rescued by the lifeboat 'Tom Perry'. On the same day, the 'Vega' of Germany and the 'Janet Izat' were both wrecked on the Herd sands. These were three of the seven ships wrecked locally in that February alone, and a disturbing number of items in the wreck register bear the legend 'never afterwards heard of'.

58. The ferry 'Tynemouth' arriving at North Shields about 1900. On Friday 20th August the ferry was taken from this prosaic shuttling to and fro to become one of the boats used for the treat for the poor children and old people of Newcastle. The 'deserving poor' marched in a procession headed by the band of the Wellesley Training Ship, followed at intervals by the bands of the Newcastle and Gateshead workhouses. They embarked from Newcastle, got off at the South Pier and the children played on the sands until after five. The event was marred for two lads, who fainted 'probably due to the excitement', 'the strong sea air', and 'a weakly state of body from privation'.

59. The lifeboat 'Bedford' at the coble landing. She was built by Lancelot Lambert at his Lawe shipyard. Miss Bedford bequeathed £1,000 to the Tyne Lifeboat Society trustees for the building of a lifeboat to be named 'Bedford' in memory of her brother who had been an engineer with the Tyne Improvement Commission. The boat was launched on 21st December 1886. She was called out three weeks later, on 11th January 1887, to the assistance of the schooner 'Earl of Musgrove' which had gone ashore on the rocks at Spanish Battery Point. The boathouse at the coble landing was built with the remainder of the money Miss Bedford had donated, and was known as Bedford House until its demolition in 1936.

60. Wood's Quay with the paddle tug 'Ulysses' and twin-crew tug Plover, taken from the Ferry Landing in 1910. Wood's Brewery originally stood here and was supplied with water from the old pit shaft at the Deans. This again stood on the site of the original works of Isaac Cookson, the Alum House from which Alum House Ham derives its name. Wood's Quay was private property and access to it was through an arched passage beside Alum House Ham. Saltwell Lane was near here, the name derived from a saline spring, which was supposed to have been useful in the treatment of sore eyes. At the corner of the lane stood one of the old riverside mansions, reputedly haunted by an 'ancient lady'.

61. Corporation Quay in 1910. This was originally the Woodfields and Subscription Brewery Quays and formed part of the property taken over with the old Brandling junction line. The Railway Company sold it to the corporation in 1861 and shortly afterwards they developed the area but it never fully realised the expectations of its promoters, probably in consequence of its restricted area. A jetty was built to facilitate a direct service from Mill Dam to London, but this was started and withdrawn in 1866. The Borough Surveyor submitted a plan for a fish market at the Mill Dam in 1867, but the scheme was abandoned and North Shields stepped in.

62. The Mill Dam Gut in 1910, with Harton Colliery staithes to the right. In the centre is a boat from which is being loaded potatoes and the horse and cart wait on the left for the sacks. A steam crane used to run further to the left. The Mill Dam was the last remains of the Mill Dam Creek. This had been the entrance to one of the mouths of the River Tyne and up to the 1750's it still filled with water from the Tyne at high tide. It had also been called the River Branin. This had been largely filled in as relief work for the unemployed after the Napoleonic wars but the gut was not filled up till the 1930's.

63. The Mill Dam ferry landing about 1900, showing the floating landing for ferry boats running to Newcastle and intermediate stations which was established in 1862. This was probably taken from the ferry itself as there is a certain amount of 'camera wobble' but the Mill Dam Customs House can be seen behind the landing stage. The building, designed by the then Borough Surveyor, Mr. Thomas Clemence, cost £3,000 to build. It was opened on July 23rd, 1864, and represented much to the new borough as at last it could have a share in the river trade previously monopolised by Newcastle. It fell into disuse but the building is still with use and is being renovated by the local Arts and Live Music Association, the price of the original building being one percent of the renovation costs.

64. As South Shields had raised both money to supply tanks and soldiers to man them, at the end of the First World War the Council was offered a tank and accepted. A redundant tank was fixed in position in an enclosure at the Lawe on 18th June 1919. It stands beside another wartime souvenir, one of the Sebastepol guns, on the far left of the photograph behind the man in his shirt sleeves. Also to the left is one of the beacons, with the groyne to its right. The first Lawe beacons, two poles with triangles on top, were put in position about 1800, and the present brick pillars which you see in the photograph, date from 1832. John Turnbull charged £60 for the two.

65. The old Redwell Lane in the late 1920's, showing the bridge for the Marsden Railway. Redwell Lane is marked on the first Ordnance Survey map of the area (1858), and seems to have been just a rough road from Redwell Pond to Marsden Bay, passing on the north side of the original Marsden Inn. By 1936 the Coast Road was completed, the Marsden Inn had moved house to a spot on Lizard Lane parallel with the Grotto, and there was a holiday camp on the right hand side of where this photograph was taken. Redwell Pond and Farding Lake are now fading memories, but locals and tourists still make their way down the steep steps to Marsden Bay.

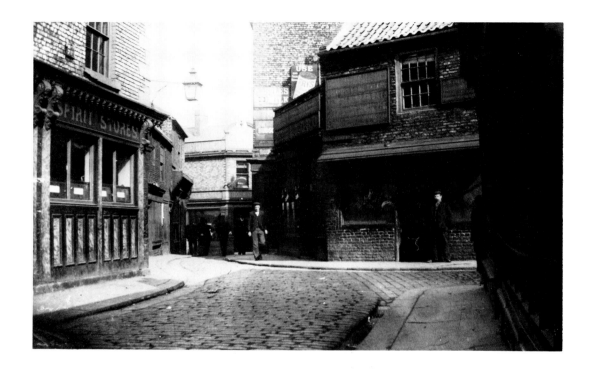

66. Where West Holborn merged into East Holborn about 1900. The old hall in West Holborn, once a mansion owned by a wealthy shipowner, was by this time let out into tenements and partially occupied by a public house. The house had a strange reputation; on one of the grand mantelpieces were the marks of two bloody fingers and a thumb. No amount of old fashioned elbow grease or new chemical cleaner could eradicate them. One person who tried was visited by the ghost of a tall handsome lady in white, with a scarlet waistband, who glided from a closed door to the window. Beetles and other vermin such as infest graves were hooked up out of the window seat by her family. They also saw the ghost of a soldier on the landing at the head of the stairs.

67. The lodge of Salmon's Hall. Thomas Salmon, first town clerk of South Shields, also gave his name to Salmon's Quay and Salmon's Ballast Hill. The hall and the lodge, now gone, stood near Manhaven, an inlet in the coast between Frenchman's Bay and Marsden Bay. The hall had originally been called Marsden Cottage, and must have been quite old for on 30th December 1809, Mr. William Barrass of that address came of age, and 'Sumptuous entertainments were given to the tenants of South Shields and Gateshead'. Thomas Salmon had a coble which lay in Manhaven, and which he used frequently, and in the winter of 1884-85, John Salmon wrote a book on this ancient type of boat, which contains practical items as well as anecdotes.

Ballroom, Marsden Grotto.

68. Marsden Grotto Ballroom in the 1920's. The person who really put the Grotto on the map was Peter Allen, who followed in Jack the Blaster's footsteps and despite opposition from the excise men, made the Marine Grotto a public house and putting his experience as a foreman in a nearby stone quarry to good use, extended the caves under the rocks. The Ballroom had been excavated by 1848, complete with the carved heads. At first it was left open to the wind and weather but by 1875 the floor and orchestra had been constructed from portions of wrecks. The door was cut out of a ship's rudder and thickly studded with ship's nails, while the heavy iron ring of an anchor served as a knocker.

69. Marsden Rock in 1896, though the earlier map-makers called it Marsden. The steps to the top of the rock are clearly shown on the far left, and in 1903 combined choirs made the ascent for a religious choral service. It was also a popular place for miner's games of Pitch and Toss and various other gambling activities. The Velvet Beds and Camel's Island are to the north-west of Marsden Rock. Near Camel's Island there are the remains of an old quay. Miss Flagg was of the opinion that this was a Roman Quay but as no research has been carried out on this it must remain something of a mystery. The remains can still be seen at a low tide.

70. Marsden Grotto about 1896. The steps down to it can just be seen on the top right hand corner of the photograph. The earliest mention of what is probably Marsden was in 1215, when the men of Harton, Westoe and Whitburn pillaged the wreck of the King's ship 'Falcon'. The first documented entry giving the name Marsden Rocks is in 1775, and records a sham battle between two groups of young men from North Shields. In 1782 an old miner from Allen Heads, popularly known as Jack the Blaster, made his home in the caverns. He and his wife arranged refreshments for the visitors who were attracted to the spot. By 1834 a cottage had been built there and steps have been cut in the rock to make it easier for visitors.

71. Coming back from Trow Rocks in the 1920's. To the right is what is now Ladies Bay but was shown as Graham's Sand on the 1855 Ordnance Survey map. Jacob's Well and the Fairies Kettle are also shown between this and Frenchman's Bay. Mr. Wallis of Westoe wrote down the story of the Fairies Kettle which was actually a circular hollow in a large cave which was only accessible at low tide. Legend has it that it once contained a golden cup and after a hazardous adventure a young man gained possession of it and brought it to the chapel of St. Lawrence at Westoe. After consideration, the priest took it to Durham and gave it to the shrine of St. Cuthbert. The Tyne Commissioners had undertaken to preserve the famous cave but a heavy fall or rock, partly due to heavy quarrying nearby, destroyed it completely.

72. The Nest, the old thatched cottage near Trow Quarry as it was in 1909. The cottage was the home of the first on site foreman for the building of the South Pier. There were quite a number of these cottages put up by the workers, as when they came here in the 1850's, there were few building regulations and no Medical Officer of Health. These must not be confused, however, with the rows of buildings called the Bents Cottages, which were built for the pitmen working at Westoe Colliery. The Nest was quite close to the old borough boundary stone which was to the south of the road running from the Broadway down to the Trow Car Park.

73. Bents House, about 1900. The original house was built in the early eighteenth century as a homestead for Bents Farm, but the Bents House known to older readers was built on this site in the latter part of the eighteenth century by John Hill (who was a member of St. Hilda's Four and Twenty from 1758-1795) after the plan of an Italian villa. It was built for Mr. Carlen, the descendant of a Flyingdale (Yorkshire) family who settled at Westoe. His daughter married into the Heath family who were at one time very influential locally. There had been a footpath on the west side of the house until about 1840 when it was closed to keep the grounds of the house more select and quiet. Today the coal washer of Westoe Colliery stands on the site.

74. The Mill Dam in the twenties. By this time it had become traditional for sailors to hang around here waiting for someone to sign them on for a ship. The policeman plays a necessary part here; there were riots in 1919 and later in 1930, mainly caused by rivalry due to shortage of work. The imposing building in the far centre was originally the local customs house. The foundation stone was laid on 27th August 1863 and the building was opened on 18th July 1864, both events marked by great ceremony typical of the day. The Tyne Commissioners made a journey down the river in state barges to take part in the proceedings at the opening. After many changes in use, it is now being re-opened as the centre for the local Arts and Live Music Association.

75. The South Marine Park about 1890, giving a view of the Wouldhave Memorial, slightly to the left of centre, the Groyne on the far left, and Tynemouth on the horizon. The Groyne, with a warning bell and light, was built in 1882, and the Wouldhave Memorial was unveiled in June 1890, at the same time as the Marine Parks were opened. The memorial was originally supposed to have been a commemoration of Queen Victoria's Jubilee, but judging by the tone of the letters to the Gazette, the public was much more concerned that it gave prominence to the efforts of Wouldhave and Greathead than the Jubilee. The memorial was designed by J.H. Morton, a prominent local architect, who used Hebburn stone for the whole design.

76. The old baths and wash-houses near Cuthbert Street, which were built in 1854 and demolished in 1906 when Derby Street Baths were built. The local council must have been quite enlightened to have built public baths so early, and in what was to be such a densely populated area. The first Ordnance Survey map of the town shows that the next houses to the south-east were those of Westoe Village, and nothing at all due east between the baths and Trow Sands. A well and a water works stand close by, with a sandstone quarry and Laygate Mill, which ground corn, to the south. To the north, however, stood the St. Hilda Pit and to the west and farther north the busy riverside. By the time the building was demolished the farmer's fields to the east had for the most part gone.

77. The old pond in Harton Village looking north, in 1908. Harton was a separate village with its own parish council until 1st November 1901. The site of the present Harton Village is slightly north of the older one, and the ruins of the original village are marked on the first Ordnance Survey map of 1856. The story, given to Mr. Coroner Graham in August 1904 by one of his jurors, was that some 150 years ago a French ship with a plague-stricken crew was driven ashore at what is now Frenchman's Bay. They got to the beach and made their way to the village of Harton. The plague killed off the inhabitants of the village and the only way that the disease could be exterminated was to burn the houses to the ground.

78. Brinkburn and Deans area about 1900, showing the footpath from the Deans to Harton Back Lane. The houses in the background are part of Stanhope Road; this can be said with confidence even though it is not marked on the photograph, for these would be the only houses laid out like this in the area; the well worn path which the girls are taking comes out into Harton Lane where Moor House was and would seem to have followed, with a few deviations, the route of Temple Park Road. Another path branched off to Mortimer Road, or Westoe Parade as it then was.

79. The bridge between Victoria and Commercial Road. The smaller of the two is the Old Waggon Way Bridge. The Waggon Way was actually to St. Hilda's Colliery and this appears to have run down to the South Shields branch of the North Eastern Railway by the 1850's but had originally joined the old road which ran across Holborn and reached the river at what was then known as Messrs. Brandling's Drops. This had been opened in 1810, but the first Waggon Way in the north-east had been opened in 1605. The early Waggon Ways had rails made of wood, later iron was used. A horse pulled the chauldron waggon along.

80. The Pier, about 1929. A popular walk, particularly on a fine day. The old Titan crane can just be seen at the top right of the photograph. Younger readers may be intrigued by what looks like a mini bridge sticking out into the harbour. This is in fact a landing place for the ferries which provided trips from Newcastle and trips round the harbour. The foundation stones for the North and South Piers were laid on 15th June 1854, but it was not until 1895 that they were completed; the gales of 1862, 1865, 1867 and 1868, having greatly hindered the work. If the Tyne commissioners had had their way, the public would never have had access to the new piers, but after various arguments, the High Court ruled that both locals and visitors could take this interesting walk.

81. Cleadon Park, showing the Broad Gravel Walk and Tropical House, shortly before its conversion to a sanatorium. The original building was an old farm house, which was converted into a mansion in the classical style by John Dobson in 1845. It was the home of the Kirkley-Anderson families; Mr. James Kirkley being greatly interested in local political and social life. The family was supposed to have been connected with the Ratcliffes, who were very influential in the north since late mediaeval times. It became a sanatorium in 1922, and closed as a hospital in May, 1978. Despite its age and connections with the Kirkley's and other famous families, plus the attractive Edwardian interior, it was demolished in 1981.

82. The old 'Vigilant' pub at the corner of Moor Lane in 1900. You can just see the 'Ship' on the centre left. The new 'Vigilant' stands on approximately the same site. There is a story that the 'Vigilant' is named after Punchy Stewart's Tug and the pub was called by that name as far back as the 1871-72 directory. Certainly, both the old and new premises have a painting of the tug above the door, the one on the present premises being by the famous local artist, Alf O'Brien, who at one time lived at Harton, in one of the houses which are just behind the pub in this photograph.

83. A police inspection in the 1920's by Chief Constable Scott. The first police force for the town was appointed in 1830. The chosen twelve policed the town in the winter only, and were paid twelve shillings a week, but extra pay was given if they assisted the Chief Constable on Saturday night in the Market Place. They possessed two pairs of handcuffs between them, but they all had hooks, lanterns, rattles and constable's staves. All but the chief and deputy were dismissed in 1831. These were for the first time styled 'police' and had the occasional help of deputy constables for night duty in winter. By 1839 there were four policemen, but in August of that year over 1,000 men, including nearly all the glass-makers and pilots, were sworn in as special constables in anticipation of a Chartist rising.

84. South Shields Harriers about 1916. The club will always be remembered as the inaugurators of the first Harrier Team Road Race in the world in 1904. By 1909, 27 teams comprising 250 runners were competing. The race was from the Wheat Sheaf, Monkwearmouth, to the County Hotel, Westoe. Six mounted policemen kept the road open for the finish, and a crowd estimated at over 5,000 stretched from Westoe to Quarry Lane. The race apparently lost popularity when the route was changed to a circular one, starting and finishing at Westoe. Near to where the runners are standing is Fred Wood's, a sporting pub managed by Fred, the world's champion cyclist of the 1880's who returned to South Shields and combined the careers of publican and town councillor.

85. The needlework class in Westoe Secondary School about 1913. Westoe school was opened in 1890, by J.C. Stevenson, M.P., with provision for senior boys, girls, junior boys and infants. There was accommodation for 2,000; the average attendance being about 1 800. The schools were amongst the ten largest in England at this time, but were soon filled, and have since been enlarged. The Westovian Dramatic Society was formed in 1920, originally for the exclusive membership of ex-pupils of Westoe Central School. During the war, the society became associated with the Northern Area Command, and played to troops stationed in the area. There must still be a few who can remember the teacher's strike at the school in May 1922, owing, it is said, to a 15 shilling cut in salaries.

86. The official opening of the Readhead Park on 18th May 1923 by Mr. Robert Readhead. The Mayoress, Mrs. J.G. Winskell, is planting a tree. The land for the park was given by Alderman Readhead as a thanksgiving for peace and victory on condition that certain work was done on the adjoining roads by the unemployed ex-service men. At the council meeting on the subject the use of the land for housing instead of a park was obviously an attractive proposition for certain councillors, particularly those who came from districts where 'key money' was demanded before houses were let, but they were defeated 26 to 9 and the park went ahead.

87. A carnival procession in the 1920's at the foot of Mowbray Road, showing the allotments behind the spectators, and the railway with coal waggons at the top left-hand side. There was a regular charity carnival week in South Shields between the two world wars; the one in 1927 was in July and was in aid of the Ingham Infirmary, the South Shields Institution for the Blind, and the South Shields Shoeless Children's Fund. A reception and dance was held by Councillor and Mrs. Ranson, Mayor and Mayoress at the time, on 18th July. Tickets were ten shillings and sixpence (£2.00 a week was quite a good wage at the time). Miss Lily Heilbron was carnival queen. There were street teas, a masked ball in the King's Hall, a tableaux parade, confetti battles, jazz band competitions, a decorated tram car or as the advert put it '168 hours of madness'.

88. The Reference Department in the public library about 1912. A public meeting was held in the early 1870's on the question of whether South Shields should have a public library or not. Despite opposition, the necessary two thirds majority in favour laid down by the Public Libraries Act of 1850 was gained. The new library, housed in the Mechanic's Institute building in Ocean Road, was opened in 1873, and by 1879 the Libraries Committee had decided to inaugurate a Local History Collection of books on the area, and photographs of old buildings. A museum was opened, and there were lectures in the hall upstairs, as well as lighter entertainment such as choirs and popular songsters. A new library was opened in Prince George Square in 1976, but many readers and staff will remember the Reference Library as it is here; and some of the chairs and tables are still in use.

89. The National Food Kitchen in the Castle Café, Sea Road in 1918. Towards the end of the First World War there were food shortages and therefore rationing was introduced. Food kitchens were inaugurated for poor children in England in 1918 and were a forerunner of the School Meals Service. Order is kept in the queue by a policeman not much older than the children, who no doubt thinks himself fortunate to have a steady job and not being drafted out to the trenches in France. The Castle Café, a quaint wooden building with turrets in imitation of a mediaeval castle, does not seem to have survived the Second World War.

90. The unveiling of the statue to Queen Victoria by Sir Hedworth Williamson on 7th May 1913. She was surrounded by bronze statues of naked ladies holding lamps aloft. While Victoria was held in due deference the 'Town Hall Hussies' caught the imagination of the general public. Embraced by drunken sailors, attired in various items of ladies' underwear, they charmed or disgusted both locals and visitors until the sad day in 1949 when both they and Queen Victoria were carried away, Queen Victoria to Chichester and the ladies to the South Marine Park. However, in 1980 Queen Victoria, then later two of her backing group, made a comeback to their old haunt outside the Town Hall.

91. The Good Friday Service in the Market Place in the 1920's. The first Sunday School was established in South Shields in 1807 by the Church of England. These were literally schools at first, where poor children could pick up some education. The march to the Market Place and open-air service on Good Friday was the idea of the Federation of Free Church Schools in 1851 and this has been an annual event since then, only prevented occasionally by bad weather. In 1936 16,000 children took part in the service, and it is still being kept up, despite efforts in 1959 to change the date. On their return to their respective churches, the children are each given a small gift such as an orange.

92. Trinity Church about 1900. This was built by the Dean and Chapter of Durham from designs by Salvin on the request of local people. The foundation stone was laid on 22nd May 1833 and the church was consecrated on 18th September 1834 by the Archbishop of York. Improvements and extensions took place, particularly in 1878-79 when a north and south transept were added, and shortly afterwards the corporation placed a clock and chimes in the tower and the congregation added two other bells, making a peal of six in all. One of the stained glass windows was to the memory of the crew of the 'Martin Wiener', lost in 1875. Another was for Thomas Henry Swinburne, who died a hero's death trying to save some workmen from suffocation. The church was demolished in 1980.

93. West Park, showing the lake, in the 1890's. The lake was originally a reservoir, and was drained in the 1920's. Old people's homes were later built on the site. There was something of a battle over the site of the park, and what became the Readhead Park was mentioned, but the present site was decided on and work commenced in the 1890's on setting it out. A news cutting of May 1893 mentions Peacock's Farm and notices to quit in that year. In 1953 the first two trees were planted in Mayor's Walk in the park by Councillor and Mrs. A.E. Gompertz. Armed with a new spade, they each planted a sycamore on either side of the path leading from West Park Road to the Bowling Greens.

94. The South Marine Park in the twenties during a band concert. This was obviously a popular pastime; admission was often free with the rather uncomfortable seats being two or three pence each. There was usually a collection afterwards. Mr. McVay, the Mayor's secretary for this period, filled a scrap book with programmes for concerts in both the South and North Marine Parks. One of the bands that played there was the Marsden Colliery Prize Band with a cornet duet 'Ida and Dot' among others. Voluntary contributions were required in aid of the uniform fund. The Grenadier Guards gave 'Reminiscences of the Plantation' and 'the Lost Chord' on 17th August 1920. The Bands of the Royal Scots Greys, the Seaforth Highlanders, the Border Regiment all played there, also the local bands such as the Harton Colliery Band, Spencer's Steel Work's Band and St. Hilda's Colliery Band.

95. Men testing the fire engine, before the First World War. The first fire brigade was formed in 1800 by St. Hilda's Vestry, with one fire engine. The fire chief got five guineas a year and his four assistants one guinea each. By 1839 there were four engines in the town, but they were not supplied with hose and buckets. The first official fire brigade was established in 1860 under the direction of the chief constable of South Shields. The early fire brigade galloped to the rescue until the introduction of a motorised engine during the First World War. After the Second World War the fire service became a separate entity from the police, and the auxiliary fire service which was brought in during the last war was disbanded. It was reinstituted in 1949, but finally became the victim of economic cuts in 1968.

96. Laygate Primitive Methodist Church in the 1920's, popularly known as Zion Hall. It was opened on 10th March 1899, and instead of a pulpit it had an open platform. This came in useful when it was used as a centre for the unemployed in the thirties. Colonel Chapman allowed the hall to be used free of charge, and was there when the Prince of Wales visited South Shields and the hall on 27th April 1932. Pantomimes and plays were produced here, with free admission for the unemployed; workers had to pay and this money went to the soup kitchen and the upkeep of the hall. It was also used by Eskimo Slippers Limited as a factory after the Second World War. It was demolished in 1962.

97. St. Mary's Church and Vicarage about 1906. St. Mary's Parish was created in 1860 because of the influx of population into the area on the opening of Tyne Dock. A temporary church was opened in the schools of the Jarrow Chemical Company, and service inaugurated on 13th May 1860. The foundation stone of the church was laid on 22nd October 1861 by Robert Ingham, and the new building was consecrated on the same date in 1862. The celebrated Schultze organ was given by Alderman John Williamson in July 1864, and the communion plate was presented by a committee of working men. The architect was John Dobson. Both church and vicarage were demolished in 1982.

98. Jarrow tram number 2 turning at Tyne Dock in 1928; the driver is Thomas Adams. Note the adverts for Barbours, Vaux's and Newcastle ales which despite two recessions and a world war still continue in business. Behind the tram we see Tyne Dock arches, these were constructed at the same time as Tyne Dock (late 1850's) and were one of the local landmarks until their demolition in 1977. Legend had it that the scene of the fatal attack on Nicholas Fairles by Ralph Armstrong in 1832 was commemorated by a blue stone built into one of the arches. William Jobling was later hanged and his body gibbetted for his part in the attack. The body was stolen but the gibbett stayed there until Tyne Dock was constructed.

99. Mr. and Mrs. Ambrose Flagg of Chapel House, Westoe Village, with their only daughter, Amy Celia. Mr. Flagg came to be headmaster of the Marine School in Ocean Road in 1886, he was an ardent church goer and deeply concerned with the Ingham Infirmary, an interest shared by his daughter, Miss Amy Flagg. Miss Flagg will be best remembered as the lady in the hat and trench coat, who quietly went about photo-graphing buildings and recording the history of the town. Many of the stories and facts in this book come from her notes and histories. Her work on ship building has been published by the library. She also assisted Anya Seton with background notes for 'Devil Water'.

4

INTERIOR OF THE EMPIRE PALACE THEATRE, SOUTH SHIELDS.

100. The interior of the new Empire Palace Theatre about 1899, after it had been altered. The Empire was at this time a music hall, though films did appear during the evening's entertainment, from 1905 to 1918. After the end of the First World War the policy was live entertainment until its closure as a theatre in 1933. Local stars such as Frank E. Franks put on reviews here in the early thirties, but the Empire will always be connected with Dick Thornton, the man who rose from being a pit lad to playing the fiddle at Marsden then on to owning this theatre then a chain of theatres. Among the top names on the bill at the Empire were Sir Harry Lauder, Charlie Chaplin, Marie Lloyd, Gertie Gitana, and of course the white-eyed Kaffir.

101. The Queen's Theatre shortly before its opening in 1913. The policy was first class entertainment, and, like the Empire, films were shown in between music hall acts at first. Films alternated with stage shows for a while, but by 1935 it was mainly live entertainment, with revues like 'Marvellous' and 'Laughter after dark'. This continued until the theatre's untimely end on the night of 9th April 1941, during an attack which seemed to have been directed mainly on the ship-building, ship-repairing and timber-yards of the riverside. An estimated number of 6,000 incendiary bombs fell that night, and soon the Queen's, along with Readhead's, the Middle Docks, Tyne Dock Engineering were ablaze. It was never rebuilt.

102. The corner of Waterloo Vale and Chapter Row showing Chapter Row Church and Freeman's Stores about 1920. Both churches and pawnshops have been on the decline for a while but now seem to be on the increase again; they were part of life in Tyneside when this photograph was taken. This was the second purpose built Methodist Church in South Shields; the Methodists moving first from what was the Cock Pit in Thrift Street to premises in East Street behind Lloyd's Bank, thence on to here. In 1809, tradition has it that the owner refused to sell the land for a chapel, but after falling ill he agreed to let the Methodist have the site if they would pray for his recovery.

DEPTH 5 FEET.

103. The opening of the swimming pool at the North Foreshore on 1st September 1923, by the Chairman of the Parks Committee, Alderman John Lawson. The concrete platform on the North Foreshore was the site of the World War I Naval seaplane base, and when the hangars were dismantled shortly after the end of the war it was decided to press ahead with an improvement scheme. This consisted of repairing the platform, joining it to the pier and building an open air swimming pool with changing facilities. Shops, shelters, tea rooms and tennis courts were also built.

104. The Middle Docks, showing no's 1, 2, and 3 dry docks about 1920, from the souvenir brochure of the visit of H.R.H. Prince Albert (later George VI) on 16th April 1920. The Middle Docks have been in existence since 1768, despite actions for bankruptcies against the owners in 1812 and 1819. The Middle Dock Company not only built and repaired ships at the docks in South Shields, but they also commissioned other ships to be built. The largest steamer ever built at Hartlepool, 'The Lamb' was launched in 1878 to the order of the Middle Dock Company. The number three dock was completed in 1909, to the order of J.H. Edwards, who revitalised the old docks and brought in new machinery.

105. The old Harton Village post office at night, showing the quaint old window. The post office was demolished for road widening in 1955. In 1819 mail
travelling by the Royal Mail coach took two days to
get to London, not bad for a vehicle depending literally on horse power. The earliest attempt to get news
sent quickly from this part of the country down to
London was in 1482 during Richard of Gloucester's
successful invasion of Scotland. In 1850 the postal
service in South Shields had a staff of two sisters and
one letter carrier. By 1900 there were 115 full time
staff and 26 part-timers at the South Shields branch
alone; with 17 other post offices in the borough.

106. John Wann's shop at 48 Waterloo Vale in the 1890's. He was a fruit and potatoe merchant. To the left we have the entrance to St. Hilda's Young Men's Institute. Waterloo Vale commemorates the defeat of Napoleon in 1815 and the street itself was laid out not long after this occurred. One of the old houses was pulled down in 1875 to make room for the institute. Below its foundations workmen found a series of water-worn boulders, obviously deliberately placed there. These were probably either ancient stepping stones or the stone causeway of a ford. The institute was opened in May 1876 by the Dean of Durham, Dr. Lake.

107. The original 'Wheatsheaf' at the corner of Smithy Street with the new 'Wheatsheaf' in 1901, shortly before the demolition of the old pub due to the widening of Fowler Street. In 1971 the new 'Wheatsheaf' was demolished in its turn to make way for the second carriageway of the Keppel Street carriageway. Numerous claims are made for the title of the oldest pub in South Shields; this is most likely to be the 'Ship' at Harton which has been there since 1803. There had been a pub on the site of the 'Adam and Eve' in Laygate since at least 1827 but the original building was demolished and rebuilt in the late nineteenth century. The Lambton Arms in East Street is also a possibility for the oldest surviving pub.

108. Harton Colliery in 1888. The first sod was cut by Mrs. Brandling on 10th May 1841 and the sinking was finished on 10th July 1845. Harton Colliery is famous as the site of the Pendulum Experiments carried out by Sir George Airey, Astronomer-Royal, to determine the weight of the earth. The description of the experiment sounds like something out of Edgar Alan Poe, with a free Kater's Pendulum, suspended on a knife-edge of very hard steel moving on an agate plane. In the early forties the South Shields miners took an active part in the formation of a new National Pitmen's Union; also in the 'great strike' from 5th April 1844 to mid-August 1844.

The band, taken outside the Casino, Sea Road about 1925. The band was founded in 1869 by John Dennison. He was the only member of the band who was not a pitman, the only one who could read music; indeed, some of the band could neither read nor write their native language. Nevertheless, the band soon rivalled others in the area, their first contest being at Windy Nook, near Felling, in 1874, when they did not get a mention. Not being satisfied, they challenged the winners, West Wylam, and in an exciting contest on neutral ground at Bedlington, they won. There was much betting on the match, and local pride together with money for once earned easily ensured the band's popularity.

109. The St. Hilda Colliery Band, taken outside the Casino, Sea Road about 1925. The band was founded in 1869 by John Dennison. He was the only member of the band who was not a pitman, the only one who could read music; indeed, some of the band could neither read nor write their native language. Nevertheless, the band soon rivalled others in the area, their first contest being at Windy Nook, near Felling, in 1874, when they did not get a mention. Not being satisfied, they challenged the winners, West Wylam, and in an exciting contest on neutral ground at Bedlington, they won. There was much betting on the match, and local pride together with money for once earned easily ensured the band's popularity.

110. A horse-drawn single decker bus on the market to Westoe route passing St. Michael's Church in Westoe Road in the 1890's. T. Gowans, J.P. Wardle, and Mr. Woodcock sit beside the driver. There had been a chapel at Westoe dedicated to St. Lawrence in mediaeval times but this had fallen into disuse. Dr. Winterbottom offered a site in his garden for a new church, but it was not until 1874 that definite plans were made to build a church. The foundation stone was laid on 7th May 1881, and the church was consecrated on 5th February 1882. It contains a stained glass window by Kemp, in memory of Alderman Broughton, Miss Flagg's maternal grandfather.

111. Tram number 8 in South Eldon Street in 1906. This was the opening of the service and at this angle the tram appears to have been quite a tight fit under the bridge. Temple Street is nearby, one of the few reminders of Simon Temple's meteoric career. At one time a successful businessman, he moved from South Shields to Jarrow Hall then to Hylton Castle, but his business failed and he died in obscurity. Temple Town Pit, also called the Manor Wallsend or Chapter Main Pit, was sunk in 1805 but the pit was not opened until 1810. It closed in 1829, and a blacksmith's shop was used by local primitive methodists for a time.

112. A casting from Black's Foundry being brought up Laygate Lane in the 1890's. The old Lay Farm was near here and there was also a Quaker burial ground in the garden of Robert Linton's house in West Pans Way, as Laygate Lane was then called. The register of this graveyard is preserved in Somerset House; the first burial recorded being in 1673, and the last in 1697. The ground had been preserved at least until 1817, but all traces of it had disappeared by 1900. Linton was an important man in the area, but this did not prevent Major Graham, the Deputy Governor of Tynemouth Castle, from arresting him and other Quakers at a meeting at his house and casting them into prison for a month, without any charges being laid against them.

113. Fleming's Baltic Bootshop in the early 1900's. It stood in Station Road, opposite St. Hilda's Church. The influence of the Boer War is seen in the notice 'South African field boats' on the left hand side of the window. The shop survived into the Second World War, the last definite date we have for it is 1940. Near here was the second charity school, which later became the offices and warehouses of the Tyne Plate Glassworks. Another of the many 'haunted houses' had previously stood on the site. It was known as the 'Bogle Bo House' until one daring soul discovered the cause of the strange sounds which was none other than a rolling barrel.

114. The old Harton Village Smithy, taken in the 1920's. It was demolished in 1964. Harton Hoppings or Fair was at one time thought second to none in Durham among the ordinary folk of the area, with its races in sacks, climbing greasy poles for legs of mutton, old women grinning through horse collars for tobacco or tea, catching pigs with their tails greased, and other traditional amusements. At nearby Horsley Hill, Madam Stote, related to the Fox family of Westoe, supplied local people with her salve or ointment, which was supposed to have had marvellous curative powers. Sadly, the recipe was a secret one handed down through generations and the ingredients were never made public.

115. Thomas Hogg Allan of 3, Westoe Terrace 1904 with his 4 horse power Tri-car outside Wyvestow Lodge, Westoe. The car had the old CU registration which is derived from Caer Urfa, the first known name for South Shields, given to it by the Brigantes, who lived here in pre-Roman times. It probably means 'town on the rock', the rock being the Lawe Top. Wyvestow Lodge stands on the site of a smithy, the old Crown Inn, and cottages; a photograph is in existence showing these three buildings dated 1889; these were demolished and the lodge was built shortly after. At first it was a private house, but has been put to various uses since being the Food Office during the Second World War.

116. Dolly Peel, officially a fishwife, but also a smuggler, poet, story teller, who had served in the Napoleonic wars and was also a great reader. Her expertise at story-telling came in useful while hiding her husband from the pressgang; they lived in Shadwell Street and he had numerous narrow escapes until finally captured. She was a great favourite with Robert Ingham and composed a poetical address to him on his being returned as first M.P. for South Shields. A song of hers commemorated the wreck of a Russian vessel laden with tallow on the Herd Sands. This made it appear that the wreck was a dispensation of divine providence to help them through a very hard winter and melted any qualms of conscience on the part of the locals who helped themselves to the basic material for candles.

117. A group of local boxers before the First World War with weights, Indian clubs etc. As far back as 1822 J. Johnson, 'in consequence of the solicitation of several gentlemen amateurs' gave a boxing display at Mr. Hall's in Long Row, J. Johnson being assisted by pupils from North and South Shields, Sunderland and Newcastle. Price of admittance was – front seats – two shillings; back seats – one shilling, which effectively ensured that ordinary working people could not afford admission. By the time the photograph was taken boxing was a sport for all, the man at the centre front being Isaac Ellwood, miner.

118. A horse tram in Laygate Lane, between 1900 and 1905. The first proposal for a tram service came in 1879, but it was not until 1st August 1883 that the first horse tram ran in the streets of South Shields. The route was from Slake Terrace, past St. Mary's Church, by Richard Street, into Commercial Road and thence by Laygate Lane, Green Street and King Street to the Pier. These were run by a private company which was not successful, and the service came to an abrupt halt after two or three years. At the beginning of 1887 another company was formed. This was taken over by the British Electric Traction Company, but as their tender for the proposed electric trams proved unsatisfactory, the service was taken over by the corporation in 1905.

119. The first electric tramcar to run on the Laygate to Tyne Dock route. The date is 23rd June, 1906. The last car on this route ran on 10th April 1938. The Cleadon route had the monopoly on the new trams, while the older stock was put on the Tyne Dock route. Many of the cars in use by the thirties were either second-hand and/or had been rebuilt. One successful transformation was the 'Monarch of Bermuda', with improved seating and heating. Others followed, such as the 'Robert Ingham', the 'Vespasian' and the 'Mauretania'. The last named had such a piercing hooter that someone felt it should have been renamed 'Dracula'. Curiously enough, it ran near a suicide's grave. A butcher had committed suicide and was buried with a stake through his heart somewhere in Mile End Road.

120. Tram number 45 on the Cleadon track about 1923. This service was formerly opened on 31st May 1922, tram number 41 heading a procession of cars. The public were allowed to sample the new route on 1st June and a twelve minute service commenced. We appear to be near the top of King George Road here; the Temple Memorial Park is to the left and what was then the new Cleadon Housing Estate is to the right. The last tram ran on this route on 1st April 1946, and the site of the old tram tracks is covered by the grass verge which now runs down the centre of the road.

121. The Chichester tramway crossing in 1906. In 1768 Laygate Lane ran through fields down to the Ballast Hills beside the river and even in 1850 one could stand at this spot and still be in the middle of fields and see the Laygate Corn Mill. The tramway sheds, built in 1906 by Messrs. Arnold of Doncaster from designs by Mr. Burgess, the Borough Surveyor, stand to the right of the picture, the official opening of the new service was on 30th March 1906; the procession starting from Fowler Street and consisting of cars number 7, 3 and 10. This proceeded to the top of Stanhope Road, and on the return journey a stop was made for the party to inspect the new sheds.

122. Wapping Street from the river about 1900, showing the direct ferry landing, Comical Corner and Kirton's Quay. The pile driver on the right is for Brigham and Cowan's Dock. The 'half penny dodger', or direct ferry, ran from here to the New Quay, North Shields, from 1847. In the early days it only took foot passengers and ran at five minute intervals. The new Brigham and Cowan's Dock was not opened until 1905, and must have created work for many, as not only had the new dock to be excavated by manual labour out of heavy clay, an old foundry converted, a long line of shops, warehouses and dwellinghouses demolished, and two quays, each with a pub to be replaced, but all this had to be carried out with only one narrow street (nine feet wide in places) as a means of access on land.

123. Thrift Street in 1898. One old house along here was supposed to have been haunted, and a servant girl in the part which had been turned into an inn saw spirits of both kinds. On her way down to the cellar one evening she saw an 'ancient lady' there, who made her promise to come back next evening without her candle. The girl kept her appointment, but was not brave enough to leave the candle behind. However, the ghost told her to put her hand in a certain crevice, and there she found the title-deeds of the house and a purse of money. History does not record what became of the title deeds, but the girl kept the money and left the inn to become 'a grand lady'.

124. The South End of Long Row, from Thrift Street to Burnthouse Bank, looking north with last house, in Thrift Street. Note the (chalked) graffiti and the boarded up shop behind the boy on the far right which gives a 1980's look to the scene. The boy's clothes would be acceptable today, but the girl beside him would be received with curious glances, if not downright laughter. The cobbles at the centre front deserve comment, they have obviously been laid by someone who knew his trade. 'Sir' Cuthbert Heron had a house in Long Row, about twenty feet above street level was a stone let in to the building with 'C. Heron, 1797' carved on it. Heron raised the South Shields loyal volunteers in 1798, in response to Napoleon's threats of invasion, but was less successful in his claims to noble ancestry.

125. The road at the top of Westoe Village in 1900. The death of Mr. Ingham in 1875 brought great changes to Westoe Village; among these the making of this entrance to the village in 1879; the owner of Westoe House undertaking to build the wall on the left of the picture. Note the smart young men, with their stiff starched collars and bowler hats. One of them is swinging his cane, as much as a part of the contemporary gentleman's dress as his hat. The dress of the boys in the picture is in sharp contrast to that of the boys in Wapping Street and Stob's Lane who would probably have mocked them unmercifully. The distance between their homes would have been a couple of miles at the most, but the distance between their lifestyles and hopes would have been immeasurable.

126. The newly built Stanhope House in 1886; taken from the south side. The small, struggling businessman's dream, Victorian prosperity in tangible form. When the Ingham Estates were divided up in 1878, several well-known businessmen in the town, including Mr. Henry Chapman, Messrs. J.M. and J.H. Rennoldson and Mr. J.P. Wardle, bought the fields to the east of Westoe House except the paddock attached to its garden, and laid out the southern half in the form of large houses, each standing in extensive grounds. Stanhope House was the one nearest to Horsley Hill Road, and its first owner was J.P. or John Potts Wardle, timber merchant, and Mayor of South Shields in 1859. The firm of Wardle's the timber merchants is still going strong.

127. Colley's Lane in 1910, looking south, with part of Colley's Farm. The farm house had been built between 1718 and 1768 to replace the Wilkinson's farm which had stood in the village from 1530. On the 14th March 1856 an agreement was reached between the Reverend Robert Green, J.C. Heath and Ralph Colley on the tenancy of the farm. Even in 1935 the farm still had oil lamps, and the Colley family was still there. The farmhouse was demolished in 1952 for the construction of the Marine and Technical College. Colley's Lane was originally a bridle road, the ancient salt track from South Shields to Monkwearmouth which crossed Westoe Village. The village pump stood on the left of the entrance to the lane which, before Colley's Farm was built, led through to the Wilkinson's farm yard.

128. This is the north side of Corstorphine Town in the 1890's, showing Edwards Dock Buildings. This had originally been a Methodist church. Behind this was what was originally the High Dock; the first definite mention of which is in 1778 when it was owned by Robert Wallis, then successively by the Wallis family, George Straker and James Edwards. Perhaps the most famous owner was Harry Smith Edwards, who gave his name to H.S. Edwards Street, one of the streets he built to house his employees. During this time the works expanded rapidly. After he died in 1898, the firm amalgamated with Smith's Docks, who gave up the dock in 1924, and it was then absorbed into Readheads Dock. Lamb's Cocoa Rooms are just beside the dock buildings. Notice the woman washing the sash window sitting out on the ledge.

129. Alum House and Spring Lane in 1898. Alum House Ham and the ferry landing are down on the left and the Ferry Tavern is on the far left. During the 1790's Simon Temple, the great local entrepreneur, lived at Alum House Ham near his dockyard in Spring Lane, or 'Back of the Shaft' as it was called then. It did not receive its more sophisticated title until 1849. Spring Lane was part of the original South Shields, which even in 1768, according to an Act of Parliament 'can now be held to consist of one street only, extending in length one mile and a half along the South side of the river Tyne, near the mouth or entrance there of'. This is borne out by the maps of that time.

130. Garden Lane, now Waterloo Vale, with the old Union British school on the right. This opened in 1834. It was the first non-Anglican public school in South Shields and had from the beginning the friendship and support of Robert Ingham, M.P. It was originally supposed to have been in Oyston Street, indeed the building was partially completed there but it was blown down by a gale so the Waterloo Vale site was selected. The original fees were 1d a week, later changes to 4d a week, and at first the school did not prosper, but after the appointment of Mr. John Thomas as headmaster in 1854, it flourished. On his death in May 1881, he was succeeded by his son, William Thomas, who kept this post until the school was transferred to the school board in 1900. It held its enviable reputation till the end. 'Garden Lane' would seem to date back to the days when much of this area was agricultural land but even in 1856 there were brick fields and a railway line here.

131. This is the foot of Thrift Street Bank with Broad Landing. Some of the old pubs here had curious names, for apart from a 'Black Swan' and a 'Jolly Jack Tar' there was a 'Silent Woman' and a 'Greenland Fishery'. The 'Silent Woman' had a sign depicting a decapitated woman carrying her head under her arm. Whether this was just a poor joke or a commemoration of one of Henry VIII's wives is not known. The 'Greenland Fishery' commemorates a trade which was once very important in South Shields. Vessels from the Greenland and Iceland fishing fleet came 200 vessels at a time to load salt at Shields from the local salt pans, and at the beginning of the nineteenth century Shields was a recognised centre of the whaling industry.

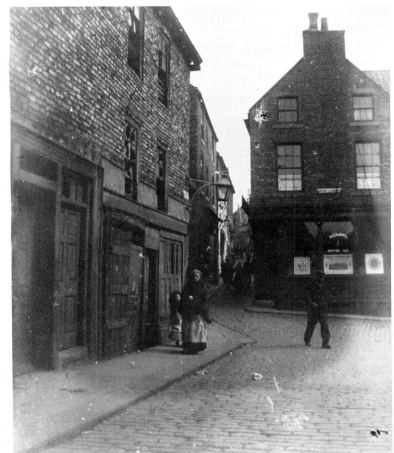

132. Fairles Quay, between Long Row and Wapping Street Brewery buildings. During the construction of the main sewer in Long Row in September 1862 an old vault was discovered under the roadway, about 20 yards east of the Broad Landing. It was built of brick, 17 feet long, 10 feet broad, 6 feet high, and contained only a small portion of coal and some wooden beams much decayed. The only visible entrance was by a hatch in the crown of the vault. It was immediately opposite where the Old Turks' Head Inn (demolished in 1838) stood, and was supposed to have been connected to it. The Turks' Head had been a very old building in 1838, so the passage could have been a link back to the days when Roman Catholic priests were smuggled into England via South Shields, or perhaps had been used for other causes. The name of the Quay is yet another link with the Fairles family.

133. The South End of Wapping Street in the 1890's. The house in the centre has been patched up with brick and either partially or wholly covered with a type of cement. The small boy, centre left, is standing at the foot of one of the narrow flights of steps up the bank which Wapping Street is at the foot of. The Methodist New Connection had a mission in Wapping Street, about 1866, but it soon outgrew its accommodation, and a new chapel was built in Heron Street. Primitive Methodism also found a temporary home in Wapping Street, in the sail-loft of Barker's Dock in 1822. The first primitive Methodist services were only held in January, 1822, but the movement grew so rapidly that by April 1823 these premises were too small, and a chapel was built in Cornwallis Street. It was built on part of St. Hilda's Glebe, and was known as the Glebe Chapel. When the congregation moved off to Westoe Road, they took the name with them.

134. Numbers 66 and 68 Wapping Street in the early 1920's. Note the variety of footwear of the boys. The shop was then owned by Anthony Wallace, but had gained a nickname which stuck until it was demolished 'Split raisin's'. Apparently an old man called Cooper had kept the shop and was so mean that he would cut a raisin in half to obtain the correct weight — and no more — for a customer. He did, however, let one of our readers leave his bicycle there when he went over on the ½d ferry to North Shields to work each day. The window cleaner is busy at number 68, Thomas Brennan's Lodging House, and on the far left is Comical Corner where the ½d ferry landed (actually a penny by the time this was taken).

135. This is Shadwell Street at the foot of Long Bank in 1898. To the right we have the wooden staging supporting the way to Corporation Quay. Rubbish and contents of the privy middens were taken up here to be placed in barges and dumped out at sea. At first sight the houses appear to be derelict but far left is a woman at a window. William Stodart, Minister of the Protestant Dissenters of South Shields, built houses here, in the eighteenth century. In the early part of the eighteenth century Shadwell Street was the home of Dolly Peel, also Sir William Hamilton, who vowed that as an act of thankfulness after his safe arrival from a terrible voyage from Hamburg, never to let the sun shine on him again. He stayed indoors, wearing away the floor of his room, until his death in June 1681.

136. This photograph, taken about 1890, is one of the oldest in the library's collection. It shows what was till the mid-1930's the oldest house in South Shields. The crest on the far left over the door shows the royal arms of the period, when Henry VIII also claimed to be King of France. It is supposed that the building was the appointed place for the collection of the customs duties, which in those days went into the private coffers of the ruling sovereign. It was certainly close to Custom House Quay, also in Shadwell Street, which got its name from the fact that the customs boats lay there awaiting in coming vessels.

137. This photograph, taken in 1892 by Mr. Hodge, shows Wapping Street with Marshall's Quay and the corner of Union Lane. Union Lane commemorates the union of the English and Irish parliaments in 1801. The men on the left have the 'cheese cutter' caps popular at this time. Below the poster at the centre of the picture there is a small post box. The name Marshall's Quay probably commemorates T.D. Marshall who had a general smith's business which was in Wapping Street. He later went on to acquire part of the old Wallis Yard near the Coble Landing and built 10 wooden and 99 iron vessels, among them the 'Star' which was claimed to be the first iron paddle-steamer to be launched in the Tyne. The firm moved to Willington Quay on Mr. Marshall's retirement in 1859.

138. Above: this is Fowler Street showing the corner of Smithy Street in 1900. These buildings will shortly be demolished for the widening of Fowler Street. W. Donaldson is apparently not only a fruiterer but according to the notices supplies rabbits and has live poultry always in stock. There was a smithy in the street in 1871, kept by H. Watson, at number 5, R. Rippon the builder was at numbers 17 to 18 and Mr. E. Tate, huckster, was at number 11. However by 1881 he has moved. R. Rippon is still there, with W. Hull, chimney sweeper at number 35, and A. Carlberg the butcher has moved in too. By 1930 we have C. Barber the wringer repairer, A.F. Singer, costumier, and Smallman's Limited, the pawn-brokers. In the early days anything moveable was pawnable; sheets, cooking utensils, shirts etc., they had special long thick pins to fasten the details on to the clothes they took, these must have played havoc with anything fine.

Below: Fowler Street corner in process of widening for electric tramways track in 1900. Nothing of what you see here remains, first the buildings advertising Runcieman's mail carts, then later St. Thomas' Church which you can just make out behind, then the old masonic lodge beside it, and shortly after the other shops to the left of the picture. The original St. Thomas' had been opened in 1819, but it was demolished and re-built in 1877. It was closed in 1963 and de-molished in 1965; the east window filled with stained glass in December 1887 by Alderman John Readhead, in memory of his wife was by August 1965 just a gap letting in the summer sun. The foundation stone of the Masonic Lodge was laid on 27th August 1862 and it was opened on 9th March 1863. It was later used as a shop but the emblems of the craft were still there until its demolition.

139. Westoe Road looking south in 1925 with the old Marsden railway bridge. The Glebe Church is just behind the bridge on the right. Soon, it too will go, and Westoe Secondary School, just up the bank on the left side after the bridge, is closing too. The sinking of Whitburn Colliery was commenced in July 1874 and in the autumn of that year sanction was obtained from South Shields Corporation for the construction of a railway from the old Stanhope and Tyne line to the colliery, crossing Westoe Lane (now Westoe Road) and other streets. Probably they used the line of the old Ballast Railway which ran across Westoe Lane, to pass Harton Cemetery to the Bents.

140. This photograph, taken about 1889, shows a large casting from Black's Foundry in West Holborn being transported to Sunderland about 1889. The 'Westoe Tavern' is in the middle distance of the first reference to it, was built in 1828 but it was not until 1829 that it was known as the 'Westoe Tavern'. It was probably rebuilt about 1841, when William Easton was licensee. The original licensee had developed gardens around the site and Easton did much to popularise them; he also sold tickets for the annual ploughing matches at Cleadon Park. The removal of the Cricket Club from Clay Path Lane to its new field at Wood Terrace brought a good deal of sporting interest to the tavern. It was rebuilt as the County Hotel by Robert Henderson in 1893, and given this name because the original suggestion for the formation of the Durham County Cricket Club was made there. Henderson founded the Westoe Gun Club and the pub was then headquarters of the Cycling Club, the South Shields Harriers and Walkers, and the Westoe Rugby Club.